RED BOOK
Wide Range Readers

Phyllis Flowerdew

Oliver & Boyd

Illustrated by Michael Charlton

OLIVER & BOYD
Addison Wesley Longman Limited
Edinburgh Gate
Harlow
Essex CM20 2JE

An Imprint of Longman Group Ltd

First published 1979
Sixteenth Impression 1998

© Phyllis Flowerdew 1979
All rights reserved; no part of this publication may be
reproduced, stored in a retrieval system, or transmitted
in any form or by any means, electronic, mechanical,
photocopying, recording, or otherwise, without the
prior written permission of the Publishers or a licence
permitting restricted copying in the United Kingdom
issued by the Copyright Licensing Agency Ltd,
90 Tottenham Court Road, London, W1P 9HE.

ISBN 0 05 003190 2

Printed in Singapore through Addison Wesley Longman China Limited

The publisher's policy is to use paper manufactured from
sustainable forests.

Preface

There are six Wide Range Readers Red Books. They can be used alone or with Wide Range Readers Blue and Green, with which they are parallel. The controlled vocabulary and graded sentence structure makes them suitable for children with the following reading ages:

7 to $7\frac{1}{2}$ years – Book 1
$7\frac{1}{2}$ to 8 years – Book 2
8 to $8\frac{1}{2}$ years – Book 3
$8\frac{1}{2}$ to 9 years – Book 4
9 to 10 years – Book 5
10 to $11+$ years – Book 6

The success of Wide Range Blue and Green Books has been proved through the years, and the author hopes that the addition of the Red series will bring pleasure to teachers and children.

Phyllis Flowerdew

Contents

The Race of Harald Gille 5
Mr Marcus Able and the Birds 13
The Land Eggs 14
A Page of Riddles 25
Northern Star 26
A Year and a Day 38
Liszt 46
The Mountain 55
Uncle Jim's Car 56
Boy or Girl 69
The Blue Bead 70
On the Track of "The Three Bears" 84
Shaggy Dog – Part 1 87
Shaggy Dog – Part 2 99
The Flying Machine 106
The Bell – Part 1 107
The Bell – Part 2 115
Another Page of Riddles 123
Seal Doctor 124
Peter the Goatherd 133
The Taffatail Tree 142

The Race of Harald Gille

Long, long ago, a stranger came to the court of the King of Norway. His name was Harald, and he came from Ireland. He had dark hair and dark eyes, and he said that he was of royal blood. His father, he said, had been Magnus Barefoot, once King of Norway himself.

Now the King of Norway liked the stranger, although he knew that he might have come to claim the throne. He thought Harald would probably make a very good king after his own death. He thought he would probably make a better king than his own son, whose name was also Magnus. His son Magnus was a lazy young man who stayed up late at night, drinking with his friends. He did very little work and took very little exercise.

One evening Magnus heard Harald talking to a man about Ireland. He said it was a beautiful, green country of mountains and lakes. He said its men were strong and swift of foot.

"There are men in Ireland," he said, "who can run faster than any horse."

Now Magnus did not like Harald, and he said at once,

"I don't believe that."

"It is true," said Harald.

"It is lies," insisted Magnus.

"I tell you," said Harald, who was getting angry. "I tell you that there are men in Ireland who can run faster than any horse."

"All right," said Magnus. "We will see. I have a very fast horse. Tomorrow I will ride it, and you shall run beside me. If you can keep up with my horse, I will give you my gold ring."

"I did not say that *I* could run so fast," replied Harald. "I said that there are men in Ireland who can do so."

"Well I'm not going to Ireland to find it out," said Magnus. "You and I will race here, in Norway." Harald did not say he would, and he did not say he would not. He rose from his stool and went to bed.

Early in the morning a messenger came to him.

"Magnus wishes to race with you," he said. Harald dressed himself in a shirt, and in trousers bound round his legs. He put on a short cloak and an Irish hat and he carried a spear.

"I have marked out the course," said Magnus. "There in the distance you can see the winning post."

"It is too far away," said Harald.

"It cannot be too far away for me," said Magnus.

Many people gathered round to watch. A chosen man gave the signal to start. The race began. Magnus, on his fine, swift horse, galloped along at a great speed. Harald kept up with him. Magnus spurred his horse on faster. Still Harald kept up with him. Magnus spurred his horse on faster, faster, faster. Harald ran like the wind, and still kept up with him.

Soon they reached the winning post – Magnus on his horse, and Harald on his own feet. They both arrived together. Harald was hardly out of breath and he looked up at Magnus in triumph.

"You did not run fairly," said Magnus. "You were clinging on to the back of the saddle all the time. My horse pulled you along."

Harald was so angry at this that he said, "We will run the race again."

"All right," agreed Magnus. "We will start here, and run it the opposite way."

A chosen man gave the signal to start. The race began. Magnus, on his fine, swift horse, galloped along at a great speed. Harald kept up with him. Magnus spurred his horse on faster. Harald passed him. Magnus spurred his horse on faster, faster, faster. Harald ran like the wind and finished the race long before the

horse. He waited till Magnus came up. Then he looked at him in triumph and said,

"Was I clinging on to the back of the saddle this time?"

"You did not run fairly," said Magnus. "You had a long start."

Harald was so angry that he could not speak.

Magnus waited a little until his horse had stopped panting. Then without saying anything he started galloping back along the course again. Harald stood and watched him. Then suddenly, Magnus turned his head and shouted,

"Start now!"

"It is not fair," murmured some of the people who were watching. "This will not be a race at all." Harald, however, was off at once, running like the wind.

"There will be no doubt about it this time," he said to himself. He ran and ran. In a few moments he had caught up with the horse and was running beside it. In a few moments more, he had passed it. In a few moments more, he had finished the course, and he sat down on the ground to rest.

As Magnus came galloping up a little later, Harald jumped to his feet and greeted him. Magnus said nothing. He turned and rode angrily away.

. . . . . .

It was not long before the King heard about the race, and he sent for Magnus and said,

"You know little about people in other countries. They do not stay up late at night, drinking with their friends as you do. Many of them work hard. They also take exercise and keep themselves strong and healthy. Now give Harald the gold ring you promised him and do not try to cheat him of what he has fairly won."

Adapted

Mr Marcus Able and the Birds

A gentleman called Marcus Able
Built the birds a feeding-table,
Filled it up with nuts and bread
And bacon-rind hung overhead,
And lumps of meat and lumps of fat
And bits of this and bits of that,
And water in a little dish
For them to drink if they should wish,
And scraps of grain and piles of seed –
Just everything that wild birds need.

Soon winter passed and then came spring,
And all the birds began to sing.
They sang to Mr Marcus Able
To thank him for the feeding-table.

The Land Eggs

This is an old story from the Isle of Man. The Isle of Man is a small green island in the middle of the Irish Sea. It is famous for its water wheel and its cats. Its water wheel is the largest in the world. Its cats are born without tails and are known as Manx cats.

. . . . . .

There was once a fisherman called Sayle. He had a large family of boys and he was very poor. He went fishing every day, but he never had a very good catch. He also left his lobster pots in the sea each night, but he hardly ever caught a lobster. The only thing that seemed to do well was the apple tree that grew beside his cottage door. It bore a good crop of small, sweet, rosy apples.

One day Sayle put a few apples in his boat, to eat while he was fishing. He steered the boat out between the rocks and he threw out his net.

After a while he heard splashing in the water beside him.

"That sounds like a very big fish," he thought. Then, to his surprise, a head appeared. It was the head of a girl with long, flowing hair, and eyes as blue as the sea. It was a mermaid. Sayle had often heard people say that there were mermaids living round the coast of the island, but he had never seen one. He could not think of anything to say to her, but he held up one of his small, sweet, rosy apples. She took it and began at once to munch it with her pearly white teeth.

"This is nice," she said. When she had finished it she swam gently round the boat and flicked her shining tail a few times. Then she said,

"Please give me another one of those land eggs."

"Land eggs!" laughed Sayle. "Those are not land eggs. They are apples from the apple tree beside my cottage door." He gave her another one, and she ate it and swam round a little more. Then she flicked her shining tail and swam deep down below and disappeared.

In the same moment, Sayle saw that his net was brimming over with fish. There were enough to feed his family and enough to sell in the market square.

"The mermaid brought me luck," he thought, but he said not a word about her to anyone.

The next day he went out fishing again. He put a few apples in his boat, and he steered it out between the rocks.

Very soon he heard splashing in the water beside him. There was the mermaid again. She swam gently round the boat, flicking her shining tail a few times. Then she clung to the boat with one hand, and said,

"Did you bring me any land eggs today?"

"Yes I did," replied Sayle, "though they are not really land eggs. They are apples from the apple tree beside my cottage door."

"I call them land eggs," said the mermaid. She ate the apple and swam round the boat and flicked her shining tail a little more. Then she smiled, and held up her hand for another apple. When she had eaten it, she dived and splashed and swam deep down below and disappeared.

In the same moment, Sayle saw that his net was brimming over with fish, and he knew that the mermaid had brought him luck again.

From that day, everything seemed to go well for the Sayle family. The father caught so many fish in his nets, and so many lobsters in his lobster pots, that he was soon able to save some money. He and his wife bought a good, milking cow, and a few fine sheep. The children in the family had plenty to eat, and they grew into tall strong boys.

"The Sayles are lucky," people said. "Everything goes right for them." But the father went out fishing every day as usual, and he always took a few small, sweet, rosy apples for the mermaid, but he said not a word about her to anyone.

Time passed and the boys grew up and the father grew too old to go fishing. Sometimes one of the boys took the boat out and another left the lobster pots in the sea, but the luck seemed to have gone. The boys hardly ever caught any fish, and the lobster pots were always empty. The cow gave far less milk, and the sheep grew weak and thin. The family became very poor again and people began to say,

"The Sayles are very unlucky these days. Nothing goes right for them."

The only thing that still did well was the apple tree that grew beside the cottage door. It still bore a good crop of small, sweet, rosy apples.

At last the boys went away and joined the herring ships. But one of them stayed at home to help his mother and father. His name was Evan. One day as he went out to fish he saw a mermaid sitting on a rock. She had long flowing

hair, and eyes as blue as the sea. Evan felt afraid. He had often heard people say that there were mermaids living round the coast of the island, but he had never seen one. He steered the boat quickly between the rocks and pretended not to look at her, but she called out,

"How is your father? He never seems to come here now." At first Evan was too surprised to speak. Then he said,

"He's well, thank you, but he's rather too old to go fishing now – and there are hardly ever any fish to be caught these days."

The mermaid smiled and said,

"Perhaps you'll be coming again." Then she slipped gently into the water and disappeared.

When Evan reached home, he said to his father,

"What do you think I saw while I was out fishing?"

"What did you see?" asked his father.

"I don't suppose you'll believe me," said Evan. "I saw a mermaid, and she asked how you were." The father's face lit up with pleasure and surprise.

"Perhaps our luck will come back again," he said. "Next time you go fishing Evan, take a few apples with you. The mermaid likes apples."

Next day Evan put a few apples in the boat and went out to fish. He steered the boat through the rocks, and looked all round for the mermaid.

Soon he heard singing and a gentle splashing, and there she was! She leaned over the boat and stretched out her hand for one of the apples.

"Ah! Land eggs! Thank you," she said.

"They are not land eggs," explained Evan. "They are apples from the apple tree beside our cottage door."

The mermaid ate the apple, and swam round the boat flicking her tail a few times. Then she ate another apple and swam round a little more. Then she dived and splashed and swam deep down below and disappeared.

In the same moment, Evan saw that his net was brimming over with fish, and he knew that the mermaid had brought luck to his family again.

For a long time after that, Evan went fishing every day. He always took a few apples for the mermaid, and he always caught a lot of fish.

His lobster pots were always full of lobsters. His father's cow gave good rich milk, and the sheep grew strong and fat. Everything went well.

Then, as Evan grew older he wanted to see more of the world than the Isle of Man, and he made up his mind to join a ship and sail to foreign lands. The mermaid was upset when he told her.

"I'll come back one day," he promised, "but before I go I will plant an apple tree above the bay where you live. Then when the apples are ripe they will drop into the sea and come to you by themselves."

So Evan planted an apple tree above the bay, and when the apples were ripe they dropped into the sea for the mermaid. But whether she ever came to look for them, and whether Evan ever came back to look for her, no one will ever know.

*Adapted from the folk tale
recorded by Sophia Morrison*

A Page of Riddles

Q. Why was the little Egyptian boy worried?
A. Because his daddy was a mummy.

Q. Have you heard the riddle about butter?
A. Better not spread it around.

Q. When can you spill a full glass and spill no water?
A. When it's full of milk.

Q. How can your father avoid falling hair?
A. By jumping out of the way.

Q. Where does Saturday come before Thursday?
A. In the dictionary.

Q. What happened to the man who couldn't tell putty from porridge?
A. His windows fell out.

Northern Star

The fishing boat was called *Northern Star* and she belonged to Olav's father. She was old and black with tar, because she had belonged to Father's father before him. In those days she had been a sailing ship, but Father had long ago fitted her up with a diesel engine and a wooden wheel-house. So the mast now held a lantern instead of a sail, and the boat could chug across the water without ever having to wait for a wind.

Olav and his family lived in Norway in a small fishing village on a narrow, twisting arm of the sea. Olav loved *Northern Star* and would not have changed her for any other boat, not even for one of the gleaming modern boats that sometimes slipped into harbour, or passed in the distance on the open sea.

He was allowed to play in *Northern Star* when she rode at anchor. He would clamber over the seats and climb up into the wheel-house. He would shout orders to an imaginary crew. He would pretend to cast out the nets, and then to haul them in, laden with fish. It was a game of which he never tired.

In the evenings when Olav was getting ready for bed, Father would take *Northern Star* out fishing. With him would go Olav's big brothers, Henrik and Per. Sometimes Olav would go with them just for a treat, and he looked forward eagerly to the time when he would be big enough to go every night.

But suddenly in the summer when Olav was nine, *Northern Star* began to show signs of wear. Some of her boards began to rot. The wheel-house roof let in the rain. She sprang a leak in her side.

Father missed several nights' fishing while he was busy repairing her. Then, when he had made her fit to sail once more, things started going wrong all over again.

Henrik was lucky enough to get a job on another man's boat, and Per took a few days' work helping in a shop from time to time, but Father's money grew less and less because of all the repairs that *Northern Star* needed.

One Sunday at lunch time, when the family were sitting down to their meal of cold fish and cheese and bread, Father said sadly,

"It's no use. *Northern Star* is too old to sail now. She has given good service for many years but her timbers are rotting and her joints are cracking open, and we cannot safely patch her up any more."

For a moment no one said a word, but gloom settled over the table like a great black cloud, and Olav gulped so hard that he nearly choked.

Then Mother sighed and murmured,

"Poor old *Northern Star*. It will be sad to see her go."

"I suppose we shall have to sell her and buy another boat," remarked Henrik.

"We shall never be able to afford another boat," said Father. "We shall get very little money for *Northern Star*."

Olav's heart sank. Sell *Northern Star*! Let someone else have her, and repair her and look after her and take her out to sea! He could think of nothing worse. Then straight away he heard something worse, much worse.

"She's only good for breaking up," put in Per.

"True," agreed Father. "She's only good for breaking up."

Northern Star to be sold and broken up! That was a thought that Olav could not bear. He gulped, and big tears slid down his cheeks on to his meal of cold fish and cheese and bread.

Next day *Northern Star* was propped up on the beach and Father put a notice on her side.

"For Sale" it said.

"Father," asked Olav in a husky voice. "Why would anyone want to buy a boat just to break her up?"

"He could use parts of her in other boats," explained Father. "He could use the engine and the mast and some of the better pieces of wood, and perhaps the wheel and the seats. The rest would only be used for firewood."

Firewood! *Northern Star* used for firewood!

Just then a man came along. He stood and gazed at *Northern Star*. He gazed for a long time. Then he said,

"May I look inside?"

"Certainly," said Father, and he held the man's arm as he stood on a box for a step and clambered over the side. Father hoped he might sell *Northern Star* to someone like this, straight away, but Olav hoped and hoped that no one would ever buy her.

"She's a fine old boat," remarked the man when he came out again. "They don't make them like this these days." Then he said

goodbye and was gone.

Olav breathed a sigh of relief.

"Do you think he'll buy her?" he asked.

"I shouldn't think so," replied Father. "He looked a townsman – not the sort to want an old boat."

Other people stopped and stared from time to time, but no one else wanted to look inside. No one else even asked any questions about *Northern Star*. People could see for themselves that she would never sail again.

A week passed – two weeks, three weeks. Father joined another fishing boat at night, and slept for part of the day as he had done in the past.

Only Olav was left now, playing near *Northern Star*, to try to sell her. He knew it was bad of him, but he did not mean to try to sell her at all. How could he try to sell *Northern Star* to someone who would break her up for firewood?

"Good morning," said a voice, and there was the man who had looked at *Northern Star* on the first day.

"So you haven't sold her," he said.

"No," replied Olav.

"I'm so glad. I thought I might have been too late. Will you go and fetch your father for me? You can tell him Mr Hansen wants to buy his boat."

Mr Hansen expected Olav to run off eagerly. Boys usually liked running messages, but this boy did not move. He just stood there looking sad and rather sulky. Mr Hansen was a very kind and understanding man.

"You're fond of her," he said. "You don't want to sell her, do you?"

Olav swallowed hard and shook his head.

"You know she's too old to sail any more,

don't you?" said Mr Hansen. "Well, if I didn't buy her, someone else would. And if someone else bought her he'd probably break her up. I'm not going to do that, you know."

"You're not?" gulped Olav, speaking at last. "You're not going to break her up?"

"Oh no," replied Mr Hansen. "I have a much better idea than that."

Then Olav ran home like the wind. He wanted Father to sell *Northern Star* quickly to Mr Hansen, before anyone else came along to buy her, though what Mr Hansen was going to do with her he could not think. He wasn't going to sail her. He wasn't going to break her up. What was he going to do?

Olav could not think what Mr Hansen would do, and if Father knew, he kept it a secret. Meanwhile Mr Hansen sent two men with a lorry, and a trailer for a boat. Father and Henrik and Per helped them to put *Northern Star* onto the trailer behind the lorry. Then sadly they and Mother and Olav watched *Northern Star* trailed away up the narrow street and out of sight.

She had gone. *Northern Star* had gone. Olav felt very sad, but at the same time he felt very glad that the beautiful old fishing boat was not going to be broken up and taken apart.

Then, one Saturday afternoon two weeks later, Mr Hansen came in a car and took Mother, Father, Henrik, Per and Olav for a ride. He would take them to the town of Larsen, he said, where he lived. But when they came to the edge of the town he stopped by a big open gate.

"This is our new park," he said. "It used to be a field, but we are making it into one of the finest parks in Norway. Come for a walk in it."

They all stepped out of the car, and walked along between green lawns, and newly-dug beds set out with gaily-coloured flowers. They passed young trees and bushes and a paddling-pool for little children. Then they came to a sand-pit and swings and a climbing frame and –

"*Northern Star!*" shrieked Olav. "*Northern Star!*"

There stood *Northern Star* on a stretch of green grass. Her wheel-house had been freshly painted, and her mast pointed up to the summer sky. She had been scrubbed and cleaned, and there was a white gangplank leading up from the ground, with a handrail on one side.

Northern Star looked so big out of the water. She looked so beautiful. She smelled of new paint and old tar and the salt sea.

Then Olav saw that there were children scrambling over the seats and climbing up to the wheel-house. Some were shouting orders to an imaginary crew, and some were pretending to cast out nets and then to haul them in, laden with fish. They were town children, and some of them had probably never seen a fishing boat before.

"A real boat for them to play in," said Mr Hansen. "Your *Northern Star* is going to give a great deal of happiness to a great many children for a long, long time, Olav."

"Yes," whispered Olav. For a moment he stood watching, and feeling so full of happiness and so full of sadness. Then he looked up to Mr Hansen and said, "May I go aboard her?"

"Of course," replied Mr Hansen. "Every child on her thinks he or she is the captain, but we know that *you* are really the captain, don't we?"

Up the gangplank ran Olav and over the side. He clambered over the seats and climbed into the wheel-house. He walked on the deck and stared up to the top of the mast. He watched the children and listened to their shouts. They all looked so happy and sounded so happy.

Olav felt that *Northern Star* must feel happy too, for what better ending could a beautiful old fishing boat have than this?

A Year and a Day

This is a very old story from Cornwall.

Once upon a time there lived a girl called Jenny. She was very pretty, and she liked to arrange flowers in her hair and look at herself in the pools of water. She was a dreamy girl too, and did not much like the idea of having to earn her living. But one day when she was about fourteen, her mother said,

"Jenny, you must walk to the next village and see if you can get work at one of the big houses there."

So Jenny set off across the fields in the sunshine. Soon she came to four cross roads. She looked at each in turn, but she was not at all sure which was the right one. She sat down on a big stone, wondering which way to go.

After a while a handsome young man suddenly appeared before her.

"Can I help you?" he said kindly.

"Thank you sir," she replied. "I am looking for work."

"What kind of work can you do?" he asked.

"Anything I am asked to do," said Jenny.

"Do you think you could look after a little boy?"

"Yes. I am very fond of children."

"Well," said the stranger. "My little boy has no mother to look after him. I want someone like you to come and care for him. Will you come?"

"How long would you want me to work for you?"

"A year and a day."

"Yes," agreed Jenny. "I will come, but first I must go back home and tell my mother."

"I will send a message to her," said the man. "I know where you live and I have sometimes seen you putting flowers in your hair, and looking into one of my pools." Then he added,

"Before you come, you must promise to stay for a year and a day."

"All right," agreed Jenny. "I promise to stay for a year and a day."

The man took the road that led to the east, and Jenny followed him. They walked and walked a long, long way, and the man did not say another word. On and on they went, until at last Jenny felt so tired that she sat down on a bank and began to cry.

"Are you tired?" asked the man kindly. "Never mind. Rest a little."

After a while he picked some small leaves that grew among the grass and he dried Jenny's eyes with them. At once she felt better. She was no longer tired, and everything around her seemed different, as if she had stepped into another world.

The country was more beautiful than any

she had ever seen. There were hills and valleys covered in flowers. There were clear rivers and waterfalls. There were people walking or resting in the grass. There were people singing songs and telling stories. Everyone was dressed in green and gold, and the sun shone with a new and brilliant light.

Jenny's new master had changed too and now he also wore green and gold. He led her into a large house where the furniture was made of ivory. It was set with gold and silver and gleaming pearls and green emeralds and shining red rubies. He led her through many rooms, each just as wonderful as the others. Then he said,

"Here is my little boy's room."

Never had Jenny seen anything like it! The room was hung with lace so fine that it looked as if it were made of cobwebs. The lace was

worked with flowers and leaves and it hung like drifts of cloud in the clear light.

In the middle of the room was a little child's cot made out of a big sea shell. The light danced on it and shone on it with all the colours of the rainbow.

"Come and see him," said the man, and Jenny stepped forward and peeped into the cot.

"Oh!" she murmured, for in the cot, fast asleep, was the most beautiful little boy she had ever seen.

So Jenny's work began. She had to wash the little boy when he awoke. She had to feed him and play with him and take him for walks in the garden, and put him to bed at night. She could not have wished for a better life, and she was as happy as could be. Her master was very kind to her and the time passed very quickly.

Somehow she forgot all about her old life, until suddenly one morning she awoke and found herself back in her own bed in her mother's cottage. A year and a day had passed, and her work had ended.

She felt very puzzled and unhappy, and everything at home seemed strange to her. She could not remember leaving the beautiful house and her master and the dear little boy. She did not know how she had come back home. She sat up in bed and rubbed her eyes, while her mother called out to a passing friend,

"Jenny's back home! Jenny's back!"

Several women from the village came into the cottage to welcome her.

"Where have you been?" they asked.

She told them of the wonderful countryside, and the beautiful house. She told them of her kind master and the dear little boy.

"It can't be true," said some of the women.

"She's making it all up."

Then an old, old woman from the village came in.

"Jenny, bend your arm," she said, "and put your hand on your hip." Jenny did so.

"Now," went on the old woman. "Say this – 'may I never stretch my arm out again if I am telling lies'."

"May I never stretch my arm out again if I am telling lies," said Jenny.

"Now try to stretch it," said the old woman. Jenny took her hand from her hip and stretched her arm out without any trouble at all.

"It's truth she has told us," said the old woman. "She must have been carried away by the Small People who live under the hills."

So Jenny settled down at home once more, but she never felt quite happy again and she often thought about the kind man and the dear little boy. Sometimes she wandered past the four cross roads and looked for the wonderful country and the beautiful house, but she never, never found them again.

Adapted

Liszt

One evening in October in the year 1811, the people of a little village in Hungary were staring up at the sky. Ever since August of that year, a comet had shone over Europe. It was like a brilliant star with a tail of fire, but tonight it shone more brightly than ever. It was so brilliant that it seemed to light up the whole sky, so that even the little wooden huts and houses of the village could be plainly seen.

"It's a bad omen," said some people. "It foretells wars and sickness and hunger."

"It means that the end of the world is near," said others.

"It's a good omen," said some people. "It foretells happiness and good harvests."

"It can hardly be a good omen for the little Liszt baby born this evening," remarked someone else. "His mother fell down a well only a few days ago. She has not yet had time to recover from the shock."

"So her baby is here is it? Is it a boy or a girl?"

"A boy. They are calling him Franz."

Just then Adam Liszt, the father, came out for a little fresh air.

"Hullo Adam. How's the baby? How's your wife?" The village men crowded round him.

"Let's go to see the gypsies," suggested one. "Perhaps they will tell you about your son's future. This is certainly a most unusual night to be born. Look at the sky. Look at the strange light."

So Adam and a few of the men walked to a field just outside the village, where a family of gypsies were camping. The night was warm for October and the air was as soft as silk.

An old, old gypsy woman sat by the camp fire, watching the flames leap and dance. Her face was brown and wrinkled, and her hair hung in grey wisps from under a scarlet head scarf.

"It's a strange and beautiful night, mother," began one of the men.

"It is indeed," she answered.

"Our friend here has a son born not an hour ago," said a neighbour of Adam's, and he pushed Adam Liszt forward to ask his baby's fortune.

The old gypsy stood up and asked him a few questions. Then she stared into his eyes.

"Your son has a great future before him," she said. "I cannot tell you what he will do, but he will become famous throughout the land. Franz Liszt you say he is called. It is a name that one day everyone will know."

. . . . . .

For several years it did not look as if the old gypsy woman could possibly be right about Franz's future. It did not look as if he would have a future at all. He was pale and thin, and often very ill. His mother and father had to take great care of him, and they were afraid to let him do most of the things that small children usually like to do.

When he was five years old, however, his parents thought again of the comet and the old gypsy's words. "He has a great future before him," she had said. Now it seemed as if her words might be coming true after all. The little boy, Franz, had a gift for music. There was a piano in the house, and he started making up tunes and playing them.

His father, Adam, would perhaps have liked to have been a musician himself, but he worked out of doors on the large estate of a nearby prince. He was able to teach Franz to read music, but in a very few years there was nothing more left to teach him. The little boy already played like a grown-up person and he had a wonderful memory, so that he never forgot music that he had learned. People began to say he was as clever as Mozart had been as a child.

"The comet was a good omen," said Adam to his wife. He knew that Franz had a great and special gift. He knew that he would need the very best teachers of music that he could find.

Adam was too poor to pay such people, so he had an idea. He would arrange a concert for the child. Then when people heard him play and saw how gifted he was, perhaps some rich person would offer to pay for his lessons.

This was just what happened. A group of noblemen agreed to pay for Franz to have music lessons for the next six years. Adam was a sensible man. He found out that one of the best teachers of the day was called Czerny and he lived in Vienna. Vienna was in Austria. The Liszt family would have to leave their village home in Hungary, and travel to Vienna.

Adam sold his watch and his furniture. The family climbed into a stage coach and went rattling over the stony roads to Vienna. There

they rented a small, shabby room in an inn called "The Green Hedgehog". There too, they stood their old piano, the most valuable thing in their lives.

Franz was ten by this time. He was old enough to know that he wanted to spend his life making music. He was old enough to know that the best teacher he could have would be Czerny.

"I *must* have lessons with Czerny," he said.

This was not easy. Czerny was so famous as a teacher and as a composer of music that he could not possibly take all the pupils who wanted lessons with him. He was already teaching for ten hours a day. He was already using all the hours of daylight and much of the lamp-lit night as well, writing, writing music, playing, playing music.

Then one day Adam Liszt arrived at his house with the little boy Franz. They were shown into Czerny's drawing room, where his piano stood waiting.

"Please will you give music lessons to my son?" asked Adam.

"I'm afraid not," replied Czerny. "I already have too many pupils. I cannot take any more."

"But my son Franz has a special gift," said Adam. "I have taught him all I know. People say he is as good as Mozart. Please, please take him." Czerny sighed. He was tired of all these people who thought their children were so clever. He was tired of all the people who thought their children were as gifted as Mozart.

"No. I am sorry," he said. "I cannot possibly take even one more pupil."

Adam's heart sank. The family had come so far to see Czerny. Franz needed him so much.

But Franz solved the problem himself. He slipped quietly on to the piano stool. He began to play some of Czerny's own music from memory.

The two men stopped talking. Czerny listened. He was amazed. This ten-year-old boy was playing one of the most difficult of Czerny's own pieces. He was playing it as well as Czerny would play it himself. The music filled the room and echoed down into the street below. It was wonderful.

"I will teach you," said Czerny. "I shall not want full fees. Just two florins a lesson will be enough. I can see that you were born to be a musician."

. . . . . .

So the gypsy was right. Franz Liszt had a great future before him and soon he became famous, in Hungary, in Austria and in all the countries of Europe. He wrote more than a thousand pieces of beautiful music, which are still played today throughout the world.

The Mountain

I went to see a mountain,
I thought it would be high,
As high as a house perhaps,
Or a tree,
Or a church.
But no, it climbed through the clouds,
So high, so very high,
Higher than *anything* I'd seen,
And its peak was lost in the sky.

Uncle Jim's Car

Uncle Jim loved his car. There was no other word for it. He really loved it. It took the place of the family he did not have. It was a Ford Escort, still fairly new. It was blue and sleek and shining. It was a four-door model, with seats covered in grey. Its number was TKJ 93R.

He spent his week-ends cleaning and polishing it. It was the shiniest car in town. He knew every mark on it. There was a tiny dent below the back window. There was another small dent above the left front headlight. These had been there when he had bought it second hand, but it was a good car and it had been well looked after.

He spent most of the summer evenings lying underneath it or standing with his head inside the bonnet. He was tuning up the engine, he said. It was a wonderful engine. It had its own special purr, like a happy, friendly cat.

"I'd know that purr anywhere," said Uncle Jim. "Blindfold me. Let me hear ten engines all purring together and I'd pick out my own at once."

"Would you *really*?" said Carol and Barney. They called him Uncle Jim, but he was not their uncle at all. He just happened to rent a room in the old lady's house next door to them. He rented her garage too. It was an old tumble-down shed really, but it kept the precious car safe and dry.

One Friday evening Uncle Jim put his head over the garden fence and said to the children,

"I'm going to Winchester tomorrow. Would you like to come with me? Bring some sandwiches for lunch?"

"Yes please," said Barney.

"I'll go and ask Mother," added Carol. She ran indoors.

"Yes, we can come," she said a few minutes later. "Mother says she'll pack some lunch for you as well."

So on Saturday morning early the children sat in the car.

"Safety belts done up?" said Uncle Jim, and the journey started.

It was a cool, fresh morning and the car was soon speeding along the motorway.

"Hear the purr of that engine?" said Uncle Jim lovingly.

"Mm," murmured Carol. Uncle Jim's engine sounded the same as any other car engine to her, but she knew she and Barney would have to admire it a dozen times before the day was over.

"Goes like a bird, doesn't she?" said Uncle Jim.

It was about ten o'clock when they reached Winchester. Uncle Jim parked the car in a large, open car park at the back of the shops.

"Meet me here at one o'clock," he told the children. "I have one or two calls to make, so you two can wander round on your own. There's a good statue of King Alfred in the High Street, and you can go in the cathedral. It's one of the finest in England."

They walked out of the car park together. They all turned round and took a last look at the car standing in its place – blue and sleek and shining – number TKJ 93R.

"Remember where it is, won't you," said Uncle Jim.

"Yes," agreed the children. Then they went one way and Uncle Jim went another.

The morning passed quickly. The children went in the cathedral, and in a small park. They looked at the shops and bought themselves some ice cream. They spent some time in the library and they gazed at the great statue of King Alfred in the High Street.

"It's getting on for one o'clock," said Barney at last. "We'd better be going back. I must say I'm hungry."

They returned to the car park. They went straight to the place where the car had been left. It was not there.

"We must have come the wrong way," said Barney.

"I'm sure we haven't," replied Carol, "because I remember that furniture van standing opposite."

"We must have done," said Barney. "Let's try the next row."

They went up the next row of cars, and the next and the next. They saw blue cars, black cars, fawn cars, green cars, but they did not see Uncle Jim's car. They saw Ford Escorts here and there. They even saw blue Ford Escorts here and there, but they did not see Uncle Jim's blue Ford Escort.

"Let's go back to the entrance and start again," said Barney. He was very puzzled. He was sure they had gone the right way the first time.

They went back to the entrance and started again. They walked up the row of cars. They saw the furniture van again, but they did not see Uncle Jim's car. Carol felt worried. This was becoming rather like a bad dream. She had the feeling that they might go on looking for the car for ever. She was afraid they might never find it.

"There's Uncle Jim," cried Barney in relief. He would know where it was. He would remember where he had left it. The children ran up to him, but as soon as they saw his face, they knew that he was as puzzled as they were.

"I've looked everywhere," he said. "I've been in here a good ten minutes. I've looked along every row of cars in case I had remembered the place wrongly, but I know I am right. I left it here – opposite that furniture van. It's gone. Someone has stolen it."

Poor Uncle Jim. This was the very worst thing that could happen to him. His car had been stolen. It must have been stolen some time ago, because a different car was standing in its place. The precious Ford Escort, blue and sleek and shining, had been stolen. Uncle Jim's precious car, number TKJ 93R, had gone.

. . . . . .

On a Saturday morning two months later, Carol and Barney were out with Uncle Jim again. This time they went with him to the town of Reading. Uncle Jim was still a very unhappy man. The car he drove now was a Cortina he had hired from the local garage. The police so far had found no trace of the blue Ford Escort that had been stolen in Winchester.

Carol, as always these days, was looking at the number of every car that passed. She was looking for TKJ 93R. She knew it was no good looking for a blue Ford Escort. The thief would have painted it a different colour long ago.

"It's no good looking for the number either,"

Barney told her. "The thief will have changed the number as well." Barney had not much hope of the car ever being found now. Two months was a long time. Uncle Jim had not much hope either.

There was a lot of traffic in the town that day. There were a lot of people shopping too. Some of them stepped off the pavement between the slow-moving cars. Uncle Jim's Ford Cortina crawled along in low gear. Then there were traffic lights changing to red. Uncle Jim stopped. A car drew up beside him. It was a Ford Escort, a yellow one. Gloom settled on Uncle Jim. The lights changed to orange and then to green. The Ford Escort was on its way a split second before the Cortina. The purr of its engine came to Uncle Jim's ears like music.

"It's my car!" he cried to the children. "My car!"

"How do you know?" asked Barney.

"The sound of it! That purr! Don't let the car out of your sight."

The yellow car was only a little ahead, but it reached the next set of traffic lights in time to get through on green. Uncle Jim was just stopped by orange. After that he began to act as if there were no such thing as a speed limit. He wove in and out of the traffic with the yellow car still in sight.

"He's going left," shouted Barney, or "He's going right." Luckily the race lasted only a few minutes and then the yellow car went over the bridge and followed the road that led out of town. It was easier for Uncle Jim to keep it in sight now. He kept behind it, but not too close.

"He's slowing down," said Barney after a while. The yellow car stopped outside a house on the outskirts of the town. Uncle Jim went slowly past and stopped just out of sight behind some trees. Then he and the children walked back along the path. The driver left the car and went into the house. Quick as a flash Uncle Jim touched the car just above the left front headlight.

"Yes. A tiny dent," he said. Then he looked just below the back window.

"The other dent," he said. "And look. You can see a trace of the old blue paint. This is my car all right."

"Are you going to take it?" asked Carol.

"No, I can't do that. I'll have to tell the police about it and leave it to them. They'll look inside for the engine number, and underneath for the number there." Uncle Jim wrote down the number of the house and the car, and the name of the road. Then he patted the yellow car and said lovingly,

"You'll soon be back with me, my old dear." And of course it was, for a few days later the police returned it to him.

"Finding this has given us clues to several other stolen cars in the Winchester area," they said. "The man who was driving it had bought it from someone else and had no idea it was stolen. He's given us the name of the man he bought it from, and we know enough now to lead us to the thief."

"Thank you very much," said Uncle Jim.

"It was your own good detective work," replied one of the policemen.

"It was the purr of the engine," said Uncle Jim. "Blindfold me. Let me hear ten engines all purring together and I'd pick out my own at once." Then he patted the car and said fondly,

"I can't say I like you in this yellow colour. I'll save up for a few weeks and then I'll have you put back in blue again."

Boy or Girl

Long ago in Holland, there was a rich man who wanted to build a church in the town where he lived. He could not decide whether to put a tower or a spire on the top.

When the church was partly built, he decided to go on a pilgrimage to the Holy Land. By that time, his wife was expecting a baby.

"If the baby is a boy," said the man, "finish the church with a spire, but if it is a girl, build a tower instead. Then I shall see it on my return journey when I am still far out at sea."

The months passed, and twin boys were born, so their mother had two spires built side by side on the church.

The church with its twin spires can still be seen today.

The Blue Bead

This story comes from Africa. It was first told by an African story teller many many years ago. It is about a magic spear, talking elephants and a strange blue bead.

. . . . . .

There were once seven brothers who married seven sisters. In a few years, they had so many little children that they began to feel their village was getting rather too crowded.

"We had better go different ways," they said to each other, "and start new villages of our own." So the first five brothers said goodbye to each other and went their different ways – to the lake-side, to the forest, to the plain. But brother number six and brother number seven had always been great friends and they wanted to be together.

"Let us go to the edge of the forest," said brother number six. "There is plenty of wood there for building a house."

"Yes," agreed brother number seven. Then he looked thoughtful and said, "Do you remember the saying 'Dogs and cats can live together in peace, but brothers can never do so'?"

"Yes, I remember," replied brother number six, "but we will try."

So they went to the edge of the forest where the grass met the trees, and they built a house. They lived in it with their families for a whole year. The two brothers lived at peace together, though their wives and children sometimes quarrelled a little.

Now brother number seven had a spear that his father had given him. It was a very old spear, and brother number seven put it along one of the roof beams, out of reach of the children. No one was allowed to touch it, not even his brother. They called it the magic spear.

Now one day when the maize was tall and ripe, brother number seven took the cattle out, and brother number six stayed at home.

Suddenly brother number six heard shouts and crackling sounds outside the house.

"The elephants are trampling over the maize," his wife cried. Brother number six jumped up and grabbed the first spear he saw. It happened to be the magic one. He rushed out of doors. He saw the crowd of elephants, trampling through the maize, breaking the stalks, and treading them under foot. They were spoiling, spoiling the whole year's crop.

Brother number six was so angry that he gave a great cry of rage, and threw the magic spear with all his strength. It stuck into the side of one of the elephants. The elephant turned and went charging away into the forest, and all the others followed him.

When brother number seven brought the cattle back that evening, he noticed at once that his magic spear was missing.

"Where is my magic spear?" he asked.

"It is stuck in an elephant's side," replied brother number six, and he explained what had happened. Brother number seven was very angry.

"Why did you have to use that spear when we have so many others?" he grumbled. "You'd better go and get it back." The two brothers became angry with each other and began to quarrel. Then after a while, brother number six said,

"All right. I'll go out first thing in the morning and look for the elephants, and ask them for your spear."

So, early next morning brother number six set off through the forest. He took another spear and a small skin bag with a maize cake in it. All day he walked, following the paths of deer and wild pigs. He went deeper and deeper into the forest, but he could not find the elephants. He could not find their tracks, nor any sign of them at all. He walked all day, and spent the night in the forest.

Then, on the next day he came to a shabby little hut with a smoky fire outside. He saw an old woman come out and try feebly to chop up some of the dead branches that lay on the ground.

"I'll cut the wood for you," said brother number six kindly. So he chopped the wood and made up the fire, and the old woman shared her meal with him.

"Where are you going, all alone in the forest?" she asked him.

"I am looking for the elephants," he replied, and he told her about the lost spear.

"If you have hurt one of the elephants, it may be dangerous for you to go near them," said the old woman. "Elephants never forget. But I will give you something that might help you, and tomorrow I will show you the way to their home."

Then she put a small, blue bead into the hand of brother number six. The bead glowed and gleamed and sparkled, even though the sun could not get through the dark trees to shine on it.

"This is a magic bead," she said.

Next morning she led brother number six to a small path that wound through the forest.

"Follow this until it divides into two," she explained. "Then follow the wider path of the two. Soon that one will divide into three paths. Take the middle one. By midday you will come to the home of the elephants. Take off your spear and your skin bag and put them on the ground. Hold the magic blue bead tightly in your hand. Then walk bravely into the elephants' village. Do not speak until they speak to you. Then tell them what you want."

"Thank you for your kindness," said brother number six, and he followed the path that wound through the forest. After a while it divided into two, and he chose the wider path. Soon that one divided into three and he followed the middle path. On and on he went, deeper and deeper into the forest.

Suddenly, about midday, he came to a huge, huge clearing, the biggest he had ever seen. The earth had been beaten down by many great elephant feet, and all round it was a kind of fence made of uprooted trees.

"This must be the elephants' home," thought brother number six to himself. It was indeed the elephants' home, for now he could see hundreds and hundreds of elephants, old ones, young ones, big ones, small ones, dark grey ones, light grey ones. On the far side of the village was a tall fig tree, and under it sat a great bull elephant with tusks white and shining and very long.

"This must be the chief," thought brother number six. He put his spear and his skin bag on the ground as the old woman had told him. He felt afraid but he held the magic blue bead tightly in his hand and he walked bravely forward. He stood in front of the chief and waited for the elephants to speak.

"Kill him! Kill him!" cried one young elephant. "He is the man who threw the spear at us." Then the chief said softly,

"Why have you come here?"

"Elephants," began brother number six

loudly. "I am sorry that I was unkind to you when you walked through my maize crop. I am sorry I threw a spear at you. I did not mean to hurt you, but only to frighten you. The spear stuck into one of you, and you took it away into the forest. It is my brother's spear and he has sent me to get it back. Please will you give it to me?"

The chief talked awhile with the elephants near him. Brother number six knew they were trying to decide what to do about him. Would they give him back his brother's spear? Or would they keep him a prisoner in their village? Would they perhaps even kill him because he had thrown the spear at them? He felt afraid, but he held the blue bead tightly in his hand and waited.

At last the elephant chief spoke to him again. "We will give you your brother's spear," he said, "because you were brave enough to come and ask for it, but first you must make two promises to us."

"What are they?" asked brother number six.

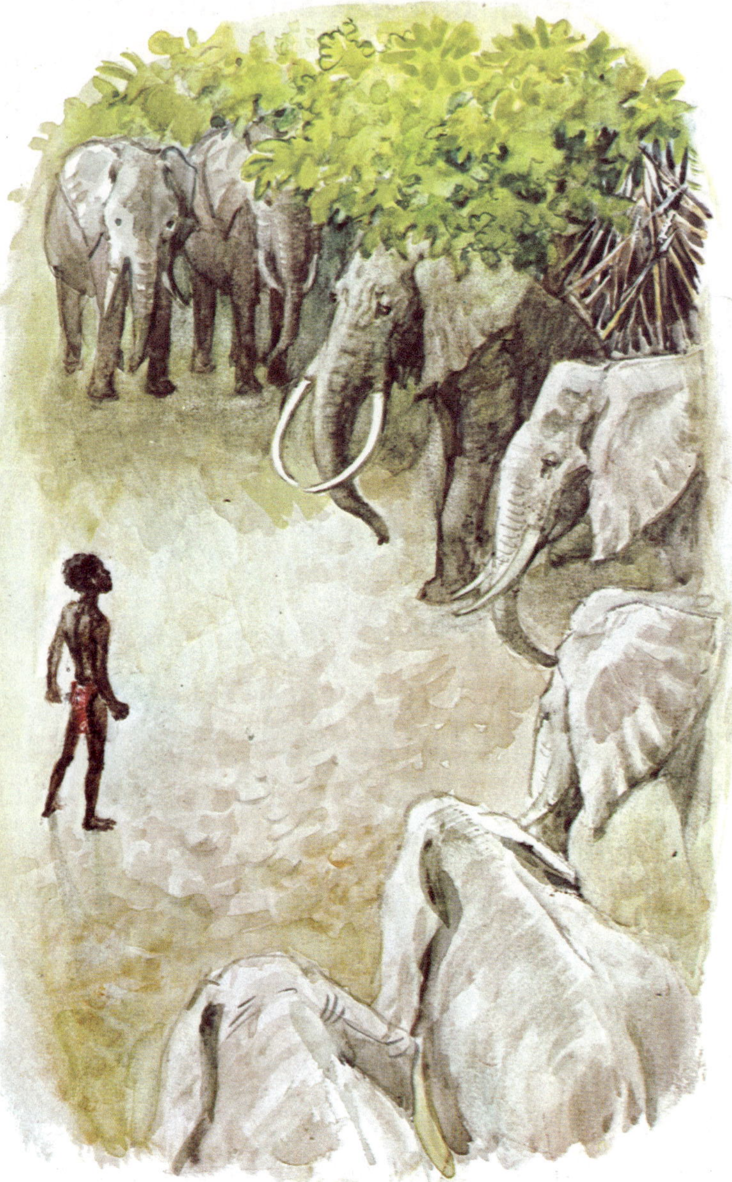

"When you are growing maize, you must build a little hut beside it. A little child must sit in the hut to keep watch. Then if we elephants come near, the child can bang an iron pot to tell us not to touch the crop. Then we shall know that you have planted the maize and that it has not grown by itself. You must teach this to your children and your children's children."

"Yes, I will do that," agreed brother number six.

"And," said the chief, "you must promise never to tell anyone how to get to our village."

"I promise," he agreed.

Then the elephants showed him a big pile of spears at the back of the fig tree.

"Choose your own," they said. Brother number six saw number seven's magic spear almost at once for it was on the very top of the pile. He took it down and thanked the elephants. He picked up his other spear and his skin bag and he went home.

It took him a long time, for he lost his way,

and he wandered in the forest for many days. When he reached home, the two families came running out to meet him, and he gave the magic spear back to brother number seven. He was pleased to have it back, and the two brothers were friends again.

"And we will not quarrel any more," they said.

But, alas – in the evening, brother number six told the families about the elephants' village, being careful not to say where it was, and he told them about the old woman and the magic blue bead. He held the bead up for them to see, and it glowed and gleamed and sparkled.

"How beautiful it is!" they said, and they passed it round from one to another, so that all could touch it and see it clearly. The two wives looked at it. Their little girls looked at it. Their little boys looked at it, until it was passed to the very youngest. This was the baby son of brother number seven and before anyone knew what was happening he had put it into his mouth and swallowed it!

Then brother number six was very angry and he shouted at number seven,

"I risked my life to get your spear back. Now you have let your son swallow my magic bead. You had better give your son to me."

"That I will not!" answered brother number seven, and in a moment the two brothers were quarrelling again.

After a while brother number seven said,

"Do you remember the saying 'Dogs and cats can live together in peace, but brothers can never do so'?"

"Yes, I remember," said brother number six. "Tomorrow I will go away and build a new house for my family in another place, as all our brothers have done."

So after that, all the seven brothers lived in their seven different villages, and as for the magic blue bead, that was never seen again.

Adapted from "Tales Told Near a Crocodile" by Humphrey Harman, published by Hutchinson Publishing Group Ltd

On the Track of "The Three Bears"

A long time ago people used to tell their children the story of The Three Bears. The story was very much the same as the one we use today, except that the bears were brothers and they lived in a castle. Another important difference was that the person who tried the bowls of milk (not porridge) and the chairs and the beds, was not a little girl. It was a fox called Scrapefoot.

Now the female of a fox is called a vixen. Vixen is a word that was often used to mean a bad-tempered woman, as well as a female fox. Some people probably called Scrapefoot a vixen, and then later, someone took this to mean a cross old woman. So, over the years, Scrapefoot the fox changed into a bad old woman.

Then one day, an English boy called Robert Southey heard the story. He had an old Uncle William who used to tell him lots of old stories; and "Scrapefoot and the Three Bears" was probably one of them. Robert Southey grew up to become a poet and an author. He wrote stories and poetry, and he wrote books about history and books about famous people.

One of his books was called *The Doctor*. It was a collection of stories, which Southey pretended were told by a man called Doctor Dove. The stories were for grown-up people, except for one. That was for children, and it was called "The Story of the Three Bears". It began,

"Once upon a time there were three bears."

It was printed in the year 1837. It told how the bad little old woman tasted the bears' porridge, tried their chairs, tried their beds, and fell asleep in the baby bear's bed.

Southey used **big print** for everything the

Great Huge Bear said. He used ordinary print for the Middle-Sized Bear's voice, and _{tiny print} for the Little Small Wee Bear's voice. He told the story in such a way that children loved it, and wanted to hear it again and again.

Many people thought that Southey had made up the story himself, and even today it is often said that Robert Southey was the author of "The Three Bears". Of course, as far as we know, he was the first person who ever had it printed in a book.

Southey told the story very much as we tell it today. So how did his bad little old woman get changed into Goldilocks? Well, people told the story, and wrote the story again and again over the years. Someone gave the old lady the name of Silver Hair. Someone changed Silver Hair into a little girl. Someone else changed the name Silver Hair into Golden Hair.

Then in the year 1904, the little girl, Golden Hair, became Goldilocks; and "Goldilocks and the Three Bears" is the story we know today.

Shaggy Dog – Part 1

Once upon a time there was a dog called Shaggy. He was quite a big dog. His coat was grey and black, and his nose was long and pointed so that he really looked very much like a wolf.

He had never slept in a house or a basket or a dog-kennel, for he belonged to a tramp, and the tramp wandered up and down the country, living on scraps of food, and sleeping in the woods or under the stars.

The tramp had given the dog the name of Shaggy, though he often said,

"If I had guessed that you were going to look so much like a wolf, I would have given you the name of Wolf instead." However, he had named him Shaggy, so Shaggy he always called him.

One very cold winter, the tramp began to feel ill. He had slept too often in wet fields, and he had not had enough to eat for a very long time. His chest hurt him so much that he could hardly breathe or speak, and he felt so shaky that it was all he could do to walk.

At last he thought to himself,

"I'll walk into the town this morning. I'll go into the hospital and ask for some medicine." So he took an old bit of rope from his bundle and he looped it round Shaggy's neck and tied him to a tree in a forest.

"Wait there like a good dog," he said. "I'll be back in an hour or two." Shaggy gave a little bark, and licked the tramp's hand. Then he sat down and watched him walk away.

The tramp walked towards the town, and after a while a lorry-driver gave him a lift, which took him quite near the hospital. The tramp found the right door and went into a waiting-room. A nurse came in and asked what he wanted.

"I just want a bottle of medicine to take away with me," began the tramp in a husky voice. Then he sank down on a chair and did not remember anything else for a long time. The nurse fetched the doctor. The doctor said the tramp was very ill, so the tramp was put to bed in the hospital.

"You will have to stay here a long time," the doctor told him, but the tramp was too ill to understand.

Meanwhile, Shaggy the dog was waiting in the forest. He was a patient dog, and he was used to going without food and water for a long time, so he did not make any fuss. He just sat quietly under the tree and waited. He waited and he waited and he waited.

Soon the morning had passed and it was afternoon. Shaggy began to feel puzzled. Why was the tramp so long? When was he coming back? He stood up and pricked up his pointed ears and listened.

Soon he heard footsteps. Was it the tramp coming back? No, the sound was too light and soft for the tramp's steps.

The footsteps, in fact, belonged to a girl called Elizabeth who was going home from school. She had rather a long walk home, for her cottage was in a lonely part of the country. She had to walk along a path at the edge of the forest where Shaggy was waiting.

When she was about halfway along the path she happened to look across at the thicker part of the forest. Then her heart stood still, for there, half hidden by a tree trunk, she saw what she thought was a wolf!

Its shaggy coat was grey and black. Its nose was long and pointed. Its ears were pricked up, listening.

Elizabeth was too frightened to cry out. She

was too frightened to run. She just turned freezing cold all over, and walked quickly on her way. She dared not even look behind to see if the wolf were following her.

Only when she had come out on to the road did she start to run. Then she ran and ran, and did not stop until she was safely inside her own house.

"Hello," said her mother. "You've been running fast. Is anything wrong?"

"No," said Elizabeth, "nothing."

. . . . . .

The next morning was very cold, and the ground was white with frost.

"Don't forget your gloves," said Mother to Elizabeth, as Elizabeth was getting ready for school. Father had gone to work early, as usual, and Elizabeth's twin baby brothers were playing on the floor.

"Hurry up, Elizabeth," said Mother, looking at the clock. Elizabeth seemed so slow this morning. Mother went to see if she were ready.

"Why, you haven't even put your coat on," she said. "You're getting late, you know."

"I don't want to go," said Elizabeth unhappily.

"Don't want to go?" said Mother. Elizabeth *loved* school. Perhaps she was not feeling well.

"Do you feel all right?" asked Mother.

"Yes."

"Then what's wrong?"

"I just don't like going by myself." Elizabeth began to mutter something about a long walk, and the forest and a wolf. Mother could not understand at all.

"Tell me slowly," she said gently. Elizabeth gave a great gulp and said,

"There's a wolf in the forest."

"A wolf!" cried Mother. She would have laughed if Elizabeth had not been so unhappy.

"There can't be!" she said. "There are no wolves in this country."

"But I *saw* one!" wailed Elizabeth.

So Mother wrapped the babies up quickly and bundled them into the pram, and walked along with Elizabeth. She saw her safely through the forest, and promised to meet her there when she came home in the afternoon.

She saw no wolf. Neither did Elizabeth, for Shaggy was lying down flat, fast asleep and out of sight. He was still asleep when Mother and the babies returned home a little later. He had waited and watched for most of the night and still the tramp had not come back.

That morning, when Mother was working in the house, she kept thinking about Elizabeth and the wolf. Poor Elizabeth! She must have dreamed it! Even while Mother was thinking this, she heard a strange, long, distant howl, and if anything sounded like the howl of a wolf, that did!

The howl, of course, was made by Shaggy. He had woken up and waited and waited, and still the tramp had not come. Shaggy was puzzled and most unhappy. He began to tug and tug at the rope.

Suddenly he slipped his head free. He gave a little yelp of joy. Now he could go and find his master. He bounded off through the trees. He sniffed his way eagerly along until he came to the road.

The scent was still strong. The tramp had gone that way towards the town. Shaggy kept his nose to the ground and hurried along in excitement. Then suddenly he lost the scent. It had vanished.

Shaggy darted quickly here and there, looking and sniffing, looking and sniffing. It was in that place that the tramp had climbed into the lorry and his scent had become lost.

Shaggy was sad and puzzled again. He sniffed

about for a long while. Then he followed the scent back to the forest, and he sat down where the bit of rope trailed from the tree, and there he waited.

By this time it was quite late in the afternoon, and Mother had already bundled the babies into the pram and walked through the forest to meet Elizabeth.

"Well," she said as Elizabeth came running to her, "I did *not* see a wolf as I came through the forest. You must have dreamed it, I think."

"I didn't," said Elizabeth, and she held tightly on to the handle of the pram and helped Mother to push it over the rough little path.

The frost had stayed all day, and the trees held out their lacy branches in winter beauty. Mother and Elizabeth trudged through the forest, and the babies in the pram gave little cries of happiness.

Suddenly, there was the sharp sound of a cracking twig a little distance away. It was the wolf! He stood for a moment like a grey-black shadow between the trees. His nose was long and pointed and his ears were pricked up, listening.

Mother and Elizabeth stopped as if they were frozen to the spot. Even Mother was startled for a second. Then the wolf came bounding through the trees to them, and she saw that it was not a wolf at all, but a big shaggy dog.

"It's a dog, Elizabeth," she said, and she patted Shaggy and stroked him. Shaggy jumped about, and licked Mother's hands, and sniffed round Elizabeth in an excited, friendly way.

Elizabeth was frightened of wolves, but she was not at all frightened of dogs.

"He's a lovely dog," she said, "but he's very thin, isn't he?"

"I think he must be lost," said Mother. "There's no dog like that anywhere round here. I must say, Elizabeth, that he does look very much like a wolf."

Shaggy the dog followed them till they came out on the road. Then he darted back to the forest and disappeared among the trees.

Shaggy Dog – Part 2

Elizabeth was no longer afraid to walk through the forest alone. In fact, she looked forward to it, and wondered each time whether she would see the shaggy dog. She did see him. She saw him the next morning, and he came up to her to be patted and petted.

She saw him again the *next* morning, and by the time she went home from school that afternoon, Shaggy was so hungry that he followed her right to the door of the cottage. Then she and Mother simply *had* to give him a good meal and a long, long drink of water.

"I'm sure he's lost," said Elizabeth. "May we keep him, Mother?"

"Well," said Mother slowly, "we will look after him as long as he stays around here. We will feed him every day and let him sleep here, but if we ever find his owner we shall have to give him back."

"Yes," agreed Elizabeth and she hoped his owner would never be found. "We ought to give him a name," she added.

"Let's call him Wolf," said Mother, and they both laughed.

So Shaggy (or Wolf) stayed with Elizabeth. He was given two good meals a day, and a bowl was kept full of fresh, clean water for him to drink. Father found a large wooden box big enough to make into a rough dog-kennel. He put some soft straw and a piece of old blanket inside it.

Shaggy (or Wolf) sniffed round it and wagged his tail, but he did not go inside it to sleep. He never *had* slept in a house or a basket or a dog-kennel, for he had always wandered up and down the country with the tramp, sleeping in the woods or under the stars.

Every morning when Elizabeth went to school, Shaggy (or Wolf) walked through the forest with her. Every afternoon he met her there again and walked home with her. But in between her going and her coming he stayed in the forest and sat down where the bit of rope trailed from the tree, and there he waited. He waited and waited for the tramp, but the tramp did not come.

Elizabeth and Mother and Father grew very fond of Shaggy (or Wolf). The babies grew fond of him, too. Father asked lots of people if they knew anyone who had lost a dog, but no one did.

"I don't think his owner will ever come now," said Father to Mother one day, when Shaggy had lived there for a few weeks. "I think Wolf will be ours for always."

"I hope so," replied Mother. "Elizabeth loves him so much."

. . . . . .

Now, what about the tramp all this time? At first he had been so ill that he had not thought of anything at all. Then, when he had become a little better, he had started to worry about Shaggy.

"It was such an old bit of rope," he thought. "Shaggy will have broken it long ago. He's clever enough to find scraps of food for himself. There's nothing I can do."

All the same, he felt very unhappy and

worried. He told the doctor about Shaggy, and the doctor said, "We'll all keep a look-out for him," but no one ever saw him.

"By the time I get out of here," thought the tramp, "Shaggy will have wandered far away. I don't suppose I shall ever see him again."

Soon he was well enough to leave the hospital. Spring was on the way and the sun was shining. It was afternoon when he left the town.

"I won't walk far today," said the tramp to himself. "I'll go to the forest where I left Shaggy. He will not be there, of course. I could not possibly expect him to be there, but I'll look for him – just in case."

By the time he reached the forest, Elizabeth had gone home from school, and Shaggy had gone with her. The tramp walked quickly through the trees. He knew just where he had left Shaggy.

The rope was still there, trailing ragged and wet from the tree, but of course there was no Shaggy. How could there be?

The tramp felt very sad, but he would not

give up the search so soon. He walked along the little path and out on to the road. He walked towards a cottage – Elizabeth's cottage. Slowly he walked past it.

Then suddenly Shaggy came leaping over the low fence like a wild wolf! He jumped up at the tramp and licked his face. He gave yelps of joy and he shivered and wriggled from the tip of his nose to the tip of his tail with sheer joy.

Mother and Father and Elizabeth saw it all from the window.

"Wolf has found his master," they said sadly, and they went out to talk to the tramp and to hear his story.

So Shaggy (or Wolf) went away with the tramp, wandering with him up and down the country, living on scraps of food and sleeping in the woods or under the stars.

That week, Father brought another dog home for Elizabeth. It was a little black-and-white puppy with a snub little nose and floppy ears as soft as velvet.

"This will be your very own dog, always," he said. Elizabeth did not think it was half so nice as Wolf, but she took it in her arms and it licked her face.

"What will you call it?" asked Mother.

"Wolf," said Elizabeth, and they all laughed.

The Flying Machine

There once was a boy who was called
$\qquad\qquad\qquad$ Jeffrey Dean.
He made a most beautiful flying machine.
Its wings were of silver, its body was green,
BUT
$\quad$ – he stuck it together with MARGARINE!

He stood on his toes on an old garden chair,
And gently, he threw the machine in the air.
It sailed on the wind. The propeller went round.
Then it all fell apart and it crashed to the
$\qquad\qquad\qquad\qquad$ ground!

There once was a boy who was called
$\qquad\qquad\qquad$ Jeffrey Dean.
He made a most beautiful flying machine.
Its wings were of silver, its body was green,
BUT
$\quad$ – he shouldn't have stuck it with
$\qquad\qquad\qquad$ MARGARINE!

The Bell – Part 1

Once, in a small town there was an old, old church with a square bell-tower. When the tower had been built, three bells had been hung in it, but two of them had cracked very soon, and only one had been used for the last hundred years.

There had been many bell-ringers through the ages, but at the time of this story, the bell-ringer was called Mr Philips and he had a boy of ten whose name was Barrie. Mr Philips rang the bell every Sunday morning to call the people to church, and he rang it every school morning to call the children to school. The bell had been rung for these two reasons as far back as anyone could remember.

On Sundays when Mr Philips went to ring the bell, Barrie sometimes walked along with him. Together they went into the silent church, and opened the heavy wooden door that led to the bell-tower. They climbed the steps inside the tower, and went into the little room where the bell-rope hung.

It was a bare little room with a queer, musty smell about it. There were a few shabby chairs, and a pile of hymn books that wanted mending.

The bell-rope hung down through a hole in the ceiling-boards and it had a long tufted handle of blue and white. Sometimes Barrie had a turn at pulling the rope, and he would hear the bell clanging out across the town. Mr Philips was never late, and he had rung the bell every Sunday and every school-day for twenty years.

Then suddenly one Monday morning he was ill. He could not ring the bell to call the children to school. Mother could not go and ring it for him because she had Barrie's three little sisters to look after.

"You can do it, Barrie," she said. "You won't mind, will you?" So Barrie left home a little earlier than usual and called in at the church to ring the bell on his way to school.

He went into the silent church. He opened the heavy wooden door that led to the bell-tower. He climbed the steps inside the tower and went into the little room where the bell-rope hung.

He had often been with his father, but now, when he was alone, it seemed so quiet and lonely and it smelled so queer and musty that he felt rather frightened. The floor creaked as he walked over to the bell-rope, and a bird or a bat gave a sudden flutter somewhere above the ceiling-boards. Barrie's heart beat fast and he longed to run out into the cool, fresh air.

He caught hold of the tufted blue and white handle of the bell-rope and pulled hard. The bell clanged out across the town. The bare, wooden room was filled with the noise, and the floor-boards trembled and shook. The bell clanged and echoed, clanged and echoed; and Barrie's heart thumped in time with it.

Soon the job was done. Leaving the bell-rope still swinging, Barrie scrambled down the steps inside the tower. He opened the heavy wooden door and closed it behind him. He walked quickly through the silent church and out into the street. Then with the bell still echoing in his ears he ran and ran, and he did not stop till he reached the school playground.

The next day was Tuesday.

"You'll have to ring the bell again, Barrie," said Mother. So Barrie left home early and called in at the church to ring the bell on his way to school. He went into the silent church. He opened the heavy wooden door that led to the bell-tower.

"I'll leave it open today," he thought. "Then I can get out more quickly afterwards." He climbed the steps and went into the little room where the bell-rope hung. It seemed so quiet and lonely and it smelled so queer and musty that again he felt rather frightened. The floor creaked and Barrie's heart beat fast, and he longed to run out into the cool, fresh air.

Soon he was pulling the rope, and the bell was clanging out across the town. The bare, wooden room was filled with the noise, and the floor-boards trembled and shook. The bell clanged and echoed, clanged and echoed; and Barrie's heart thumped in time with it.

But soon the job was done and he was telling his friends in the playground,

"I rang the bell again. My mother says I shall have to do it every day this week." He was proud of himself for doing it, but all the same he longed for Saturday to come.

So Barrie rang the bell to call the children to school. He rang it on Monday, Tuesday, Wednesday, Thursday.

Then came Friday.

"The last day," said Mother to Barrie. "Father will be well enough to start again on Sunday." But Barrie was slow getting ready that morning.

"Do hurry," said Mother. "If you are late, half the children in the school will probably be late too." So in the end it was in a great rush that Barrie reached the church and walked through the silence to the heavy wooden door that led to the bell-tower. He left the door open and climbed the steps and went into the little room where the bell-rope hung.

Although he had been there on Monday and

Tuesday and Wednesday and Thursday, he still felt frightened, for it seemed so quiet and lonely, and it smelled so queer and musty.

The floor creaked as he walked over to the bell-rope, and a bird or a bat gave a sudden flutter somewhere above the ceiling-boards. Barrie's heart beat fast, and he longed to run out into the cool, fresh air.

"Never mind. It's the last time," he said to himself. "I shall never have to do it again. I'll never come up here again, even with Father."

He caught hold of the tufted blue and white handle of the bell-rope and he pulled hard. The bell clanged out across the town. The bare wooden room was filled with the noise, and the floor-boards trembled and shook. The bell clanged and echoed, clanged and echoed; and Barrie's heart thumped in time with it.

Soon the job was done. Leaving the bell-rope swinging backwards and forwards, Barrie scrambled down the steps inside the tower.

"The last time! The last time!" he said to himself. In a moment he would be outside in the cool fresh air. But in that moment a breath of wind caught the heavy wooden door and just as Barrie reached it, it slammed shut with a loud bang! He jumped. Then he clutched at the handle and turned it. He was in too much of a hurry. He could not open the door.

He tried again. He still could not open it. Then he tried again slowly and carefully, trying not to be afraid. It was no good. The lock must have jammed or gone wrong. The door would not move. Barrie was locked in the bell-tower.

The Bell – Part 2

For a few moments he was so afraid that he pulled and tugged at the handle and shouted and yelled, but there was no one to hear him. Then after a while he sat down on the steps and tried to think quietly and sensibly.

The vicar might come into the church soon. He often wandered in and out during the week. Or Mrs Miles might come. She was the church cleaner. She might come this morning.

"The best thing I can do," thought Barrie, "is to wait quietly and listen for footsteps, *then* shout and bang on the door."

Meanwhile it was draughty on the steps. Sadly he climbed up again to the little bare room where the bell-rope hung. He sat on a chair and he tried not to think of the loneliness and quietness, and he tried not to smell the queer and musty smell. The blue-and-white-handled bell-rope was still trembling from the pulling, and the bell above the ceiling-boards was still echoing from the clanging.

Barrie picked up a hymn book and turned over the pages and looked for the hymns he liked best. He tried to sing some of them, but he did not seem to have much of a singing voice this morning. He sang and he waited and he listened. No one came. The vicar did not come. Mrs Miles did not come.

The children would be in school now. He wondered if they would miss him. They would think he was not well. They would not think of coming to the bell-tower to look for him.

But the vicar might come. Or Mrs Miles might come. He must wait patiently. He turned the pages of the hymn book again. Time passed slowly, slowly.

"Perhaps no one will come today, not even when it's time to go home from school," he thought.

He ran down the steps and shouted and yelled and banged at the door again. It was no good. No one would hear him. No one would ever hear him.

Then he had a sudden idea. The bell! The only way to make himself heard was to ring the bell. Then surely, someone would come and see why it was ringing at such an unusual time. Slowly he climbed the steps again and walked across the creaking floor to the place where the bell-rope hung.

Meanwhile, at school, Barrie had of course been missed. Miss Davies, the teacher, was puzzled, because she had heard the school bell clanging out as usual from the church and she knew that Barrie was ringing it this week.

"Has anyone seen Barrie this morning?" she asked.

"Yes," replied a boy called Tom. "I saw him go into the church to ring the bell."

"Perhaps he wasn't very well and went home again afterwards," suggested someone else. Yes, that must be what had happened.

The children settled down, and the school clock ticked on to quarter past nine, half past nine, quarter to ten, ten to ten. Barrie was forgotten now and his class were working quietly.

Then suddenly there was a great clang, clang, and the church bell rang out across the town. Some of the children were so startled that they nearly jumped out of their seats. A few of them were frightened, but some of them laughed, and everyone was very puzzled.

Miss Davies went into the playground and looked up the street. All the children followed her. People were coming out of shops and looking this way and that.

"What is wrong?" they were asking each other. "Why is the church bell ringing? There must be something wrong."

Some thought there must be a fire. Others thought the river must have burst its banks.

Someone telephoned the fire-station and someone rang up the police-station. But no one seemed to know why the church bell was ringing. The shopkeepers did not know. The firemen did not know. The police did not know.

There was one person, however, who was going to find out at once, and that was Barrie's father, Mr Philips.

"I'm well enough to go that far," he said to Mother. He pulled on his coat and was at the church door in a flash, with the vicar and Mrs Miles close behind him. They hurried through the church and pulled at the heavy wooden door that led to the bell-tower. The church was filled with the noise of the bell, as it clanged and echoed, clanged and echoed.

The door would not open. Mr Philips and the vicar and Mrs Miles all tried the handle. They turned it round and back again. They pulled and pushed at the door, but it would not move.

"It's stuck," murmured Mr Philips.

"Must be a madman up there," said the vicar. "He's locked himself in."

"I'll get Mr Black," said Mrs Miles. "He'll take the lock off the door." She hurried away, but Mr Philips went on struggling with the handle, and the vicar hammered on the door with his fists, shouting,

"Come down, come down whoever you are!"

At that moment, Barrie stopped ringing the bell, and sat on a chair to get his breath back. The echoes clanged round his head and filled his ears. Then, as they faded a little, he heard a different sound – a hammering on the door below, and voices – the vicar's voice, and his father's voice.

Down the steps he rushed, just as a policeman and a fireman arrived and Mrs Miles brought

Mr Black with a bag of tools.

"Daddy!" called Barrie.

"Barrie!" called Mr Philips.

"Don't worry," said Mr Black soothingly. "I'll soon have the lock off the door."

He fiddled with it a moment and added,

"It's jammed." He unscrewed the screws and took off the lock. Then he swung the door wide open, and out came Barrie.

But that was not quite the end of the story. A few days later when the town council had its monthly meeting, Mr Black, who belonged to it, said,

"Surely there's no *need* for the church bell to call the children to school. I'm sure the custom started in the olden days when people were poor, and had no clocks or watches in their homes. Everyone has a clock or a watch these days, as well as a radio set and a television to check them by. Is there any *need* for Mr Philips to climb up that tower every day?"

The town council talked about it and decided that there really was no need to ring the bell every day. So, the children were told not to listen for it any more. Then a week later, the school bell stopped.

Now it is only on Sundays that Mr Philips rings the church bell, and sometimes as he gets ready to leave home, he says to Barrie,

"Coming with me to ring the bell, Barrie?"

But Barrie's answer is always the same.

"No *thank* you," he says.

Another Page of Riddles

Q. If twelve make a dozen, how many make a million?
A. Very few.

Q. Why do birds fly south in winter?
A. Because it's too far to walk.

Q. What happened to the tap dancer?
A. She fell in the sink.

Q. Why do cows wear cowbells?
A. Because their horns don't work.

Q. Why does a stork stand on one foot?
A. Because if he lifted the other foot, he'd fall down.

Q. What did one ear say to the other ear?
A. Between you and me we need a hair-cut.

Seal Doctor

Linda lived in a coal-mining village in Wales. Her father had worked in and around the mines for many years. Then he became ill, and he and Linda's mother decided that a change would be good for him. They had saved quite a lot of money, so now they used it to buy a little café in Cornwall. There was a small house at the side of it, and Linda felt very excited when moving day came.

The house was in a quiet, lonely place on the cliffs, amid fields and trees. It looked out over the mouth of a river that flowed into the Atlantic Ocean. Mr and Mrs Jones and Linda worked hard getting in the stores for the café, and by the time the summer started, they had everything ready.

Then people began to come. Some of them drove up the lane in cars, and others walked along the cliffs or through the fields. They asked for coffee or cold drinks, or ice-cream or afternoon teas.

Mr and Mrs Jones and Linda were very busy indeed. But it was not only people who kept them busy.

One day Linda saw her father struggling up towards the house with a big bundle in his arms. It was white and fluffy. It had big, round, frightened eyes.

"What is it, Daddy?" she asked.

"It's a baby seal," explained Mr Jones. "It was washed up on the beach. I put it back in the sea two or three times, but it came back again and again. It wouldn't leave me. I think it believes I'm its mother."

"But it's white – like a snowball," said Linda. "I thought seals were dark and shiny."

"They are," replied her father, "but the babies have thick, white coats until they are about three weeks old."

"We'd better give it some milk to drink," said Mother, coming to look at it.

This was not so easy. The baby seal could not lap the milk as a cat or dog would do. It did not even seem to know how to suck it from Mr Jones's fingers. Then a doctor friend told them they would have to put a tube into the seal's mouth and pour the milk down the tube. It was quite a job, as the baby seal kept biting the tube; and even when the milk went into its mouth, it did not seem to know how to swallow it. However, at last the Jones family managed to get some milk into the baby. Then they had to go on feeding it four times a day.

The baby seal changed the Jones family's life quite a lot. A few weeks later another baby seal was washed up on a different beach a little further up the coast. It looked weak and ill.

"Mr Jones at the café will look after it," said the people who found it, so they took it to Mr Jones. Then when another baby seal was found, cut and bleeding on another beach, people said,

"Mr Jones at the café will know what to do with it. We'll ask him to come and fetch it."

So, before he quite knew what was happening, Mr Jones the Welsh miner became known as a kind of baby seal doctor in Cornwall.

The seals in Cornwall are usually born on little rocky beaches, sheltered by cliffs. Their mothers look after them for about three weeks, and feed them on their own rich milk.

But sometimes while the mothers are away catching fish for themselves, storms arise. The waves roll further and further up the beaches. They wash over the baby seals and pull them out into the open sea. They sweep them along with the tides, and toss them up on a different beach some time later. The baby seals are often only a few days old and have not even learned to swim. They often get cut on jagged rocks, and many of them die.

It was seals like this that were brought to Mr Jones. They were usually babies in their fluffy white coats. They had to be taught how to suck milk. Then when they were three weeks old, they had to be taught to swallow fish, and then to catch it for themselves.

When he started looking after the seals, Mr Jones knew very little about them, and some of them died because they were ill, or because the milk was not quite right for them. Mr Jones read as much as he could about them, and learned as he went along. Some of his seals were fierce because they were frightened. Some of them were gentle and playful, and liked nothing better than to lie in his lap while he stroked their heads or tickled them.

"We ought to make a pool for them," said Linda one day. So Mr Jones began digging the ground, and mixing concrete, and he made a small pool. He bought a great many sprats and mackerel from the nearest fish shop. He taught the baby seals to catch the fish which he threw to them in the water. Then as soon as they were able to look after themselves he took them down to the beach and put them in the sea.

Many of the baby seals swam happily away to freedom, but some of them stayed with Mr Jones a long time. This was because some of them were ill and needed a great deal of care.

Mr Jones was so busy looking after seals that he had to pay someone else to help Linda and her mother in the café. The seals cost him a lot too. He had to buy so much fish for them and sometimes he had to get the vet to come and see the ill ones.

More people than ever came to the café now. They came to ask for coffee or cold drinks, or ice-cream or afternoon teas. They also came as an excuse to see the seals. At first the seals were kept in a shed. Then Mr Jones put them in pens with rails round them, and people loved to lean over and look at them.

"I don't know what we're going to do," said Mr Jones to his wife one day. "We can't possibly go on looking after all these seals, but when people bring them to us, we can't turn them away, can we?"

"Oh no," said Mrs Jones. "We can't turn them away. They would just die. I wish the fish didn't cost so much."

"Some people think this is a hospital for seals," put in Linda. She thought for a moment and then added,

"Why don't we *make* it into a hospital for seals, and make people pay to come in? The money would help to pay for the fish."

"Good idea," replied Mr Jones, "but we really can't look after a café *and* a seal hospital."

So in the end, Mr Jones sold his café. He spent the money on making a better home for the seals. He also made two big pools for them. The seals came and went. Sometimes there would be seven or eight. Sometimes there would be as many as forty in a single year.

People came and went too. People on holiday came. Parties of schoolchildren came, and every year a group of children came from a school in Holland. Even then the money from the entrance fees was not enough. So Mr Jones stood a money box inside the seal house with a notice on it, saying "For the seals", and somehow he kept the hospital going.

There are still many storms on the rocky coast of Cornwall. There are still many baby seals that lose their mothers and get swept away by the high tides. There are still many seals that get cut on the jagged rocks. What a good thing it is that Mr Jones, the Welsh miner, decided to live on the cliffs of Cornwall.

Peter the Goatherd

Once upon a time there was a man called Peter. He lived with his wife and children in a small village among the forests of Germany. There he had a cottage and a herd of goats. Every morning he took his goats out to graze on a nearby mountain side. There they wandered among the rocks and stones from one patch of grass to another.

Sometimes Peter took the goats home in the evening, but sometimes they had wandered too far for this. Then he would lead them to a place in the woods where part of some old low walls were standing.

There had once been a cottage there and though it was now in ruins there was still a doorway where the goats could enter. Peter would stand by the doorway and count the goats as they went through.

One evening, after driving all the goats into the shelter of the walls, Peter found that one of them was missing. It was the prettiest goat of the herd.

"I wonder where she can be," he thought, but in the morning, when he awoke from sleep, there she was with the others.

The next evening the same thing happened; and the evening after that, it happened again. Then Peter looked carefully all the way round the wall, and he found a hole in it. It was just big enough for a goat to squeeze through.

"Tomorrow evening I will follow the goat and see where she goes," he thought.

Next evening, Peter watched until he saw the goat squeeze through the hole in the wall. Then he ran quickly through the doorway and followed her. Up the mountain went the goat, jumping from rock to rock until she came to a cavern.

When Peter found her a few minutes later she was eating corn that kept falling to the ground from above. Peter was puzzled. Where was the corn coming from?

It was rather dark in the cavern, but he could feel the corn dropping around him. He stood still and listened. He thought he could hear horses stamping and munching. He listened again. Yes, he was sure there were horses feeding above, and the corn must be falling from their mangers. But who would keep horses in a mountain in such a lonely place as this? Peter stood and wondered.

Then suddenly a young pageboy appeared and beckoned to him. Peter followed and came to a grass courtyard with walls all round it. Above the walls were great rocks and green spreading trees that almost shut out the light.

The grass was smooth like a lawn, and on it there were twelve old knights with long beards, and old-fashioned clothes. They were playing skittles, and there was no sound except the banging of the ball and the tumbling of the skittles.

The knights looked at Peter. They spoke not a word, but they showed by signs that they expected him to pick up the skittles that they knocked down. Peter was filled with fear, and he trembled, but he picked up the skittles one by one, as the knights went on playing.

After a while he noticed a jar of wine standing on the ground beside him, so he drank from it. He did not know how long he stayed there, picking up skittles. He did not know how many times he drank from the jar of wine, but soon he became so weary that he fell asleep.

When he awoke, the knights and the skittles had gone. The courtyard and the rocks and the trees had gone. He sat up stiffly and rubbed his eyes. To his surprise he found he was on the grass inside the old walls where he kept his goats at night.

But where were the goats? There was not one to be seen. He had slept so deeply that his head was spinning and he felt very strange and puzzled. He must have been dreaming, he thought, but the grass seemed longer than usual, and there were trees and new bushes scrambling over the walls.

Peter went out through the ruined doorway and began to look for his goats. He wandered over the mountain side, looking in the places where they usually grazed. But there was not a goat in sight.

"Perhaps they went home without me," he thought. "I'd better go and see." He took the path that led down to the village, and as he drew near he passed two or three people. He knew everyone who lived in the village. Yet he did not know these people. He thought they were dressed strangely too.

"Have you seen my goats?" he asked them. They stared at him and smiled a little and stroked their chins. Peter put his hand up to his own chin. To his horror he found that his beard reached down to his waist. How could it have grown so long in a single night?

He felt almost as if he had woken up into a different world. Yet the mountain was the same. The forest was the same. The houses and the gardens in the village were the same. Oh well! He would go home and tell his wife about his strange dream. Perhaps he would find the goats outside his own cottage. He felt worried and strangely sad.

Soon he came to his cottage. How shabby it looked! The white walls had become grey and dirty and there were big patches where plaster had fallen away. Even the front door had tumbled down, and when he looked inside he saw that the cottage was empty. He called his wife's name, but no one answered. He called his children's names but there was no reply.

When he came out, a little crowd of women and children were gathering.

"Who are you?" they asked.

"Who are you looking for?"

Peter thought it would seem too foolish to stand at his own cottage and ask strangers where his wife and children were. So he said the first name he could think of at that moment.

"I'm looking for Hans the blacksmith," he said.

"He died seven years ago," replied one of the women.

"Well – the tailor – Frank," said Peter.

"He has lain in the churchyard for ten years now," said an old woman. Peter looked at her. He seemed to know her face. Yes. She was one of his friends, but how different she looked! Fearfully he looked from face to face. Fear gripped his heart. Everything was so strange, so puzzling. What had happened to him?

Just then a young woman pushed her way through the crowd. She had a baby in her arms and a little girl at her side. All three of them looked very much like Peter's wife. He held out his hand to the woman.

"What is your name?" he asked.

"Mary," she answered.

"And what is your father's name?"

"Peter," she replied. "My father's name was Peter. He was a goatherd but he disappeared on the mountain twenty years ago. I was seven years old then, and I remember it well. The goats came back without him and we spent days looking for him on the mountain side. We never found him, and we never heard of him again!"

Then Peter the goatherd kissed the baby and put his arms round the woman's neck.

"I am Peter," he said. "I must have been asleep these twenty years!"

The other people stared and whispered. Then someone said,

"It is Peter – Peter the goatherd. He has come back after twenty years! Welcome home, Peter. Welcome home."

Adapted

The Taffatail Tree

A sailor, a sailor
   from over the sea,
He gave me the seed
   of a Taffatail Tree.

On Monday I dug,
   and the seed was soon sown.
On Tuesday I found that a plant
   had just grown.
Next day 'twas a bush
   of consid'rable size,
And on Thursday a tree
   – I could scarce trust my eyes.
On Friday there hung
   – it's the truth that I tell –
A dozen blue pears
   with a chocolaty smell.

The next day they burst,
  and twelve monkeys crept out,
And started to swing
  and to clamber about.

But on Sunday, quite early,
  before the sun shone,
When I looked from my door for the tree,
  it had gone!

And I *can't* find the sailor
  from over the sea,
Who gave me the seed
  of the Taffatail Tree.